The Man with the Plastic Sandwich

A Comedy

by Roger Karshner

A Samuel French Acting Edition

New York Hollywood London Toronto
SAMUELFRENCH.COM

Copyright © 1978, 1982 by Roger Karshner

ALL RIGHTS RESERVED

CAUTION: Professionals and amateurs are hereby warned that *THE MAN WITH THE PLASTIC SANDWICH* is subject to a Licensing Fee. It is fully protected under the copyright laws of the United States of America, the British Commonwealth, including Canada, and all other countries of the Copyright Union. All rights, including professional, amateur, motion picture, recitation, lecturing, public reading, radio broadcasting, television and the rights of translation into foreign languages are strictly reserved. In its present form the play is dedicated to the reading public only.

The amateur live stage performance rights to *THE MAN WITH THE PLASTIC SANDWICH* are controlled exclusively by Samuel French, Inc., and licensing arrangements and performance licenses must be secured well in advance of presentation. PLEASE NOTE that amateur Licensing Fees are set upon application in accordance with your producing circumstances. When applying for a licensing quotation and a performance license please give us the number of performances intended, dates of production, your seating capacity and admission fee. Licensing Fees are payable one week before the opening performance of the play to Samuel French, Inc., at 45 W. 25th Street, New York, NY 10010.

Licensing Fee of the required amount must be paid whether the play is presented for charity or gain and whether or not admission is charged.

Stock licensing fees quoted upon application to Samuel French, Inc.

For all other rights than those stipulated above, apply to: Samuel French, Inc.

Particular emphasis is laid on the question of amateur or professional readings, permission and terms for which must be secured in writing from Samuel French, Inc.

Copying from this book in whole or in part is strictly forbidden by law, and the right of performance is not transferable.

Whenever the play is produced the following notice must appear on all programs, printing and advertising for the play: "Produced by special arrangement with Samuel French, Inc."

Due authorship credit must be given on all programs, printing and advertising for the play.

No one shall commit or authorize any act or omission by which the copyright of, or the right to copyright, this play may be impaired.
No one shall make any changes in this play for the purpose of production.
Publication of this play does not imply availability for performance. Both amateurs and professionals considering a production are strongly advised in their own interests to apply to Samuel French, Inc., for written permission before starting rehearsals, advertising, or booking a theatre.
No part of this book may be reproduced, stored in a retrieval system, or transmitted in any form, by any means, now known or yet to be invented, including mechanical, electronic, photocopying, recording, videotaping, or otherwise, without the prior written permission of the publisher.

ISBN 978-0-573-61859-8   Printed in U.S.A.   #15050

THE MAN WITH THE PLASTIC SANDWICH, by Roger Karshner, directed by Tod Booth, Set and Lighting by Robert W. Rupp, Costumes by Saundra Rethman, was presented by Tod Booth at the Drury Lane Theatre, Evergreen Park, Ill., on January 16, 1981.

CAST

WALTER PRICE	*Frank Gorshin*
ELLIE	*Julie Crisman*
HALEY	*Edgar Meyer*
LENORE	*Mary Lynn Kolas*

REGARDING THE SET:

In the interest of flexibility and varying economic situations, the author does not wish to impose any hard-line attitudes in regards to the set. Therefore, the play may be presented in a most austere and simple manner, utilizing the bare necessities, namely, a park bench and a wire-link trash container, or it may be offered in a full-blown, realistic, park like setting.

The Man with the Plastic Sandwich

ACT ONE

SCENE 1

SCENE: *A park in Los Angeles. Day. NATURE SOUNDS.*

KEY SET PROPS: *a park bench, wire-link trash basket.*

At rise set is uninhabited. Then WALTER PRICE *enters.* WALTER *is forty five years old and is a most conservative fellow. He's wearing a sincere blue suit, a blue shirt and a blue striped tie. His shoes are black wing tips, his hose are thin black lysle—the kind the hairs stick through.* WALTER *is carrying a thin, black attache case in one hand, a brown paper bag in his other.* WALTER *approaches the bench carefully, looking around, checking out the environment. He places the attache case and paper bag on the bench, reaches into his jacket pocket and withdraws a white handkerchief which he unfolds and spreads neatly on the bench seat. He seats himself in the center of the handkerchief, takes up the paper bag and removes contents: a large plastic container of coffee, a tightly wrapped sandwich. He crumples the bag and tosses it to the ground. He removes lid from container of coffee and blows across the top of the liquid in order to cool it somewhat. Very carefully he takes a tiny sip.* ELLIE *Enters. She is attractive, twenty five, well built. She's attired in a smart, yellow dress. She's sporting a large tote bag. There is an uplifting, crisp air about* ELLIE. *She approaches the bench in a jaunty manner.* WALTER, *ignoring* ELLIE's *presence, lifts coffee to his lips and cautiously prepares to take another sip of the steaming brew.* ELLIE *spots the discarded paper bag.* NATURE SOUNDS OUT.

ELLIE. Ah HA! Caught you!!!!!

WALTER. What!? Huh!? (*He starts, spilling the scalding coffee to his trousers. He leaps to his feet, smacking his legs, attempting to pull hot wet material away from his legs.*)

ELLIE. (*Oblivious to* WALTER's *plight, bending down picking up bag*) Litter litter! Every litter bit hurts! Don't be a litter bug! (*Placing bag in trash basket*) Litter—the ruination of our natural environment. And you don't look like the type either. (*Looking around*) Nice day. They said rain too. You never know in L.A. (*Noting* WALTER *gingerly pulling pants from legs*) Are you alright? You okay?

WALTER. Yes, yes wonderful.

ELLIE. My Uncle Max had the same problem.

WALTER. (*Blotting trousers with handkerchief*) What problem?

ELLIE. He just couldn't hold his water.

WALTER. Now see here Miss, Miss—

ELLIE. Ms. But you don't look old enough for leaky kidneys. Ah, booze, huh? Too bad. After awhile it gets to you alright—everything goes.

WALTER. (*Blotting*) I don't drink!

ELLIE. It's no sin, you know.

WALTER. Now look here, Miss—
ELLIE. Ms.
WALTER. Miss, Ms., Madam, Mrs.—whatever. It's coffee! Hot, scalding coffee!
ELLIE. Oh well, coffee's just as bad. Maybe even worse. It's murder on the bladder. It goes right through you—whish! Just like that.
WALTER. This isn't a whish—this is a spill!
ELLIE. Don't be modest. I worked in a hospital once. I've seen everything. Go ahead and whish if you want.
WALTER. (*Holds coffee container aloft*) Coffee dammit! Okay!?
ELLIE. A stimulant—attacks the nervous system. None of it's any good for you. I'm organic myself.
WALTER. Miss or Ms. Organic?
ELLIE. I watch everything. Sugars, starches. No desserts ever—empty calories. And no meat. Heavens, never meat. Steroids, you know. Nothing sprayed. Whole grains. Strictly vegetarian. Are you vegetarian? No—you look meat, a meat look for sure. (WALTER *wipes down pants.*) My Grandfather was meat. Meat meat meat. He looked great till he was eighty. Then, alluva sudden, he went to hell just like that. Cholesterol. Like I said, it catches up. Are you into yogurt? You should be, you know, it aids digestion. (WALTER *seats himself on bench trying his best to ignore her barrage*) I'll bet right now that steroids are eating away at the lining of your stomach. (*Makes fingers like chewing teeth*)

WALTER. The only thing eating away at the lining of my stomach is hunger. (*Takes up sandwich*) Now—if you don't mind.

ELLIE. That's bad. (*Plops down beside him*) Mind if I join you? You should never ever let your stomach get completely empty. You should eat lightly and often.

8 MAN WITH THE PLASTIC SANDWICH

WALTER. (*Ignoring, unwrapping sandwich*) Lightly and often.

ELLIE. Do you know that they've found that most cancer starts right there in the stomach?

WALTER. (*Not looking at her, unwrapping sandwich*) It's comforting to know that they've located it.

ELLIE. Right down there in the little old tummy-tum-tum. You don't look the type.

WALTER. For cancer?

ELLIE. For litter. (*Catching WALTER as he's about to throw crumpled sandwich wrapper to ground*) Ah ah ah ah! (*She snatches wrapper from his hand, places it in trash basket*) Say, I'll bet you're a banker. Right?

WALTER. I'm a Clinical Engineer. Or was anyway— (*Vain attempt to eat sandwich*) Now, if you don't mind—

ELLIE. I'm a member of the Sierra Club.

WALTER. I was going to ask, are you a member of the Sierra Club.

ELLIE. That's the reason I'm heavy into litter.

WALTER. Too bad you're not heavy into light conversation.

ELLIE. I hiked thirty six miles last weekend. I saw a snake. I just love snakes.

WALTER. That figures.

ELLIE. They have cute little faces. Backpacking is great. It's wonderful for the legs. I have great calves. Just like a rock. (*Thrusts out her leg over his legs*) Here, take a feel!

WALTER. No thanks.

ELLIE. C'mon, go ahead.

WALTER. No! No I don't want—I can tell, you're in great shape!

ELLIE. I used to be in better shape. That's when I was going steady and doing it all the time.

WALTER. Doing what? Oh, doing it. (*Beat*) Doooing it!

ELLIE. Great for the abdominal muscles. Makes those little ridges. (*Pressing stomach*) But lately I'm soft. I went through EST, too. They yell at you—terrible things. One instructor called me a shit. It cost me $375.00. I think self-awareness trips are great. Getting into social stuff. Ecology, nature. And animals. I have six cats. I couldn't keep track of them so I named them all Harold. I had a dog once, too, but he got hit by a good humor truck. I think all those bells distracted him. It was terrible. He had the right of way too—he was in a cross walk. Do you come here often?

WALTER. Once in awhile. For peace and quiet.

ELLIE. You meet the most interesting people here. Yesterday I met this real cute guy—neat hair, moustache, green eyes—just like out of one of those cigarette ads. But he got fresh though. Wanted me to do it right here, in the park, in broad daylight. Can you imagine?

WALTER. It would have been great for your stomach muscles.

ELLIE. See that tall building over there? (*She points, he looks*) That's where I work. Edwards, Milliken, Stone and Katz. Legal. I'm on the twelfth floor. (*Pointing*) There! The window with one of the slats missing from the venetian blind—that's me!

WALTER. (*Peering*) I can't tell.

ELLIE. Count up twelve, then over five to the left.

WALTER. I'll take your word for it.

ELLIE. It's a nice office. I just got a new selectric typewriter. You know—changeable balls? I go for the pica type. Are you a corned beef?

WALTER. I'm a pastrami.

ELLIE. Let me see. (*He peels back bread, she peers in*)

10 MAN WITH THE PLASTIC SANDWICH

Pastrami, corned beef—they both look the same to me. Meat—ugh! There's a lot of fat in that. I've been there for over three years now. I'm going for paralegal. (*Withdrawing a pint of yogurt from bag*) I have a great boss. He never hits on me. He's married. His whole family's on his desk.

WALTER. It must be a big desk.

ELLIE. Their pictures, silly. (*Offering him spoon of yogurt*) You want a bite of yogurt?

WALTER. (*Holding up sandwich*) No thanks, I'm not heavy into enzymes. Say, aren't there other benches in this park?

ELLIE. Stay here, you're not bothering me. Anyway, I like you. You have a cute face.

WALTER. Like a snake's?

ELLIE. Do you mind if I ask you something personal?

WALTER. You mean up till now it's all been surface stuff?

ELLIE. Do you always dress like that?

WALTER. No. Sometimes I don't have the coffee stains.

ELLIE. Basic blue. It's so, it's so . . . basic.

WALTER. I've always been basic blue. I was a basic blue baby. I drive a basic blue Chrysler. I have a basic blue wife. Everything I touch turns to basic blue. Now, if you don't mind, for Chrise sake, I'd like to finish my pastrami before it turns basic purple.

ELLIE. Do you have sexual hang-ups?

WALTER. You're amazing, you know that? Really amazing. How can you talk this way to a perfect stranger?

ELLIE. It's easy.

WALTER. It doesn't bother you?

ELLIE. No.

WALTER. Well, it bothers me.

ELLIE. That's because you're a basic blue and I'm a basic yellow.

WALTER. And you put them together and they make basic green. So what the hell does that mean, if we had kids they'd be leprechauns? What is this!

ELLIE. It's a matter of personality. Everybody has a basic color. Everyone's a basic something. (*Pointing off*) Like, take that guy over there for instance. A basic red.

WALTER. (*Looking*) You're sure?

ELLIE. I'd bet on it. He's got a hot look. Firey. And see that guy going there?

WALTER. Yeah.

ELLIE. A green—for sure a green.

WALTER. From the way he walks I'd say basic magenta.

ELLIE. Definitely green. Just like you're a blue. And your color reveals so much. I'll bet you wear blue synthetic underwear.

WALTER. Alluva sudden I feel basic naked.

ELLIE. I'll bet you never run around the house with it all hanging out.

WALTER. Ah—you'd be surprised. The very first thing I do when I get home is loosen my tie.

ELLIE. Are you into group sex?

WALTER. If I'm into synthetic underwear how the hell could I be into orgies?

ELLIE. Sometimes people like you are deceptive. On the surface conservative, shy. But deep down—kinky.

WALTER. My only fetish is little girls in parks. I spread yogurt on them and then wipe it off with my pastrami! You're something, alright, really something.

ELLIE. (*Extending spoon*) Sure you don't want a bite?

12 MAN WITH THE PLASTIC SANDWICH

WALTER. No, I don't want a bite!

ELLIE. I had a boyfriend who was into kinky sex. He was a writer—creative. The stuff he thought of you wouldn't believe.

WALTER. I'd believe, I'd believe.

ELLIE. He did this thing with jello that—

WALTER. Please! Enough! Okay!?

ELLIE. Okay okay! Did I say I was into paralegal?

WALTER. Yes, you said. What haven't you said? Now please why don't you hike off like a nice little Sierra Club member and leave me here with my litter and steroids and cancer, bad kidneys and snake face? Before you showed up I was sitting here enjoying a nice quiet lapse of manic depression—now, I'm crazy altogether. So please—go someplace and boycott lettuce!

ELLIE. Boy! Are you ever an uptight person. A big blue suit full of hypertension. I hate to think of your blood pressure. (*She rises*) Look how white your fingernails are. That comes from clenching—anxiety. (*Moving behind him*) You need a good massage.

WALTER. (*Ducking*) Stay away, stay away from me, I don't need a massage!

ELLIE. (*Casually relentless*) It'll do you a world of good. You're about to explode.(*Placing her hands on his shoulders*)

WALTER. Come on now, stop that! I don't even know you, I mean—(*She begins to massage*) I mean—(*Relaxes*) A little more to the left. (*She massages*) Over a little more. (*She massages*) Now—up just a hair. Yeah, yeah—that's it.

ELLIE. (*Kneading his shoulders*) What's your name?

WALTER. (*Enjoying*) Walter. A little to the right. Walter Price.

ELLIE. I'm Ellie. Boy, are you tight. (*She bears down*)
WALTER. Ow!!!!! Easy!
ELLIE. Relax. Do you ever exercise?
WALTER. I'm not coordinated—I always pull something.
ELLIE. You ever think about jogging?
WALTER. I'm too clumsy. I'm just not athletic. I never was, even as a kid. I can't even catch a ball. I always look away at the last minute and it smacks me in the face. Over a little to the left. (ELLIE *continues treatment*) I was the only guy in the neighborhood with a ball glove that had never caught a ball—it always had that bright yellow new look to it. You have any idea what it's like standing around on the sidelines with a NEW glove!? I think my mother's to blame. She over protected me to the point I was afraid of everything. "Don't touch that wire, you could be electrocuted! Get your hands off that animal, you don't know where it's been! Walter, stand back from the edge!!!"
ELLIE. You had a neurotic mother.
WALTER. I still have a neurotic mother.
ELLIE. So you're not into sports?
WALTER. I was never into sports. I was into, "Stepping Stones."
ELLIE. Into what!?
WALTER. "Stepping Stones." A beginner piano piece. I used to play it over and over. But I never ever could get it right. My fingers would cramp up and I'd play in the cracks. But my mother insisted I had talent. It ran in the family, she said. Hell—the only thing that runs in the family is bad feet. So, while other guys were out playing ball, I was playing "Stepping Stones." Ouch! Not so hard! (ELLIE *continues treatment*)

14 MAN WITH THE PLASTIC SANDWICH

ELLIE. You're a very restricted person, Walter. I can tell from your shoulders. Your muscles are all drawn up in tight little balls. Kind of like pearl tapioca.

WALTER. I get you more as a paramedic than a paralegal.

ELLIE. (*Stops massage*) There! How's that?

WALTER. (*Moving shoulders, rotating neck*) You're stopping? That's it? You give a great massage, you know that?

ELLIE. I'm better with exotic oils.

WALTER. I'll bet.

ELLIE. I had this boyfriend once and we really used to get it on with oil. It's a real sensuous trip.

WALTER. Was that the writer?

ELLIE. A college student. He majored in Persian Architecture.

WALTER. There's a big demand for that.

ELLIE. We went together for a year before we broke up.

WALTER. What happened—the oil crisis? How many men have you known, anyway?

ELLIE. Oh tons. It's fun. I'm very open, you know.

WALTER. I'd never have guessed.

ELLIE. People should be more open. Are you into nudity? No—I shouldn't even ask. You're a sexually restricted person. Your the type who can't look below peoples' waists without blushing. No, you're not a C.W.

WALTER. A—C.W.??? What's a C.W.?

ELLIE. A crotch watcher. But not me, I want to know what's going on down there. (*Pointing between* WALTER'S *legs*)

WALTER. (*Quickly crossing legs*) Stop that!

ELLIE. You've got to learn to open up.

WALTER. Well, around you I'm staying crossed over.

Look, maybe I'm not heavy into oils and jello and I don't run around staring into peoples' flys, but I'm no sexual wallflower! I just happen to believe that nudity is for the shower and that sex is private with—ONE PERSON!

ELLIE. I agree—about the one person, that is.

WALTER. I can't believe it.

ELLIE. One person at a time.

WALTER. I'll bet you hand out numbers. Like waiting in line at Baskin Robbins. Look, Alice and I—Alice is my wife.

ELLIE. Who else.

WALTER. We have a nice compatible sex life.

ELLIE. Once a month, missionary, with the lights out.

WALTER. We don't go in for acrobatics, if that's what you mean.

ELLIE. Like I said—restricted. I can tell that from your back. Shoulder to shoulder tension. You should get into yoga. Meditation. You should expand your conscienceness. I do yoga every night. Look. (*She bends, contorts, stretches*) When's your birthday?

WALTER. July 9th.

ELLIE. Ah ha—Cancer!

WALTER. You mean I was born with steroids?

ELLIE. You were born a worrier, you keep things inside, you have intestinal problems.

WALTER. (*Laying his sandwich aside*) You think maybe the pastrami?

ELLIE. No, it's your sign. I'm a Leo. August 5th. Leos are expansive. We're open—basic yellows. Like you should learn to be.

WALTER. Right now I'm basic unemployment.

ELLIE. You? Out of work?

WALTER. Unemployment's not discriminating. It can

strike anyone, without warning. Like heart disease only worse. With heart disease you get sympathy.

ELLIE. How long you been out?

WALTER. For over six months. I can't find anything.

ELLIE. You mean, in Clinical whatever.

WALTER. Engineering.

ELLIE. It sounds very Cancerish.

WALTER. It's the planning and maintenance of hospitals and medical equipment—like that.

ELLIE. Hospitals!? You'd think there'd be plenty of work. They're always jammed and they get a fortune for everything. It cost me over $500.00 for my abortion.

WALTER. The writer, the student or the oil man?

ELLIE. A used car dealer. In and out the door. They didn't even assign me a bed. $500.00 and I didn't even get to take a nap.

WALTER. My field hasn't caught on in the West. Most of the good jobs are in the big hospitals in the East.

ELLIE. Well, maybe you'll have to move.

WALTER. I can't afford it. Why you think I'm pastrami on a park bench—because all the gourmet restaurants are crowded? A move would put me in the poorhouse for sure.

ELLIE. Anyway—it snows in the East. Being out of work is the pits.

WALTER. You've been out of work before?

ELLIE. Who hasn't? Hey, everyone gets canned one time or other. Don't get down, something will show up. Look on the bright side. You're alive, you're kind of healthy. It'll pass.

WALTER. The only thing that's passing is my savings account. Look, for you it's easy to be sickeningly optimistic. At your age unemployment's no big deal. But when you're over forty it's a big pain in the ass. "Over forty." Do you have any idea what those words mean in our society? Over forty's a stigma, it's like having leper branded into your forehead. (*Beat*) I never used to think about my age until I was fired. Now, I can't get it off my mind. It's a nightmare. (*Beat*) To make it in this society anymore you have to have red, white and blue hormones. You have to look like a perennial beach boy. You have to keep up a youth front, dress like a bellhop and grow sideburns. But what if it's not you? How do you fake it? You don't! I don't—I can't. I've tried. I bought one of those funny looking new suits and I wore it with my shirt opened down to my navel. But I felt awful, like one of those hairy idiots in the liquor ads. It just wasn't me. I took Alice dancing last week but I couldn't get into it. I'm just not a pelvis snapper. I still do the box step and actually touch my partner. And I've tried to get into rock 'n roll. I've listened to nothing but a pop station on my car radio for the past three months. Hell, I still can't distinguish the music from the commercials! I just can't fake it! I'm not twenty! I don't look like a surfer! And the only pair of jeans I own I wear to paint in. I can't hide it—I'M MIDDLE AGE! You, you're just a kid. But let me warn you. Don't get a line, don't develop a wrinkle and heaven forbid a stretch mark because you won't dare wear a bikini. You know what I am? I'm an over forty, basic blue blight on the rosy cheeks of youth crazy America. I'm no longer a human being—I'M AN EMBARRASSMENT! And if I don't find a job soon I'm going to drive off into the smog and never be seen again—ever! Because I'm angry and scared and I can't stand the thought of going through another day with a feeling of worthlessness! (*A long silence. He fidgets. Depressed.*)

ELLIE. Walter.

WALTER. Yeah.

ELLIE. You wanna do it? My apartment's right across the street.

WALTER. Are you kidding!? Are you crazy!? What kind of nut are you, anyway!!!!!?????

ELLIE. Gee, excuse me! I just thought it would help relieve your tension.

WALTER. The only thing that will relieve my tension is peace an quiet! Now—PLEASE! Lemme alone!

ELLIE *shrugs her shoulders.* WALTER *sits back indignantly, opens attache, withdraws classified section of newspaper. He pulls half-glasses from inside jacket pocket, slips them on. He snaps paper a few times in order to arrange it, raises paper, begins to read ads.* ELLIE *routs through her bag like a squirrel digging for nuts.* WALTER, *distracted, witnesses her askance over top of half-glasses with look of great incredulity.* ELLIE *withdraws pair of jogging shoes from bag, slips off her street shoes, places them in bag. She laces on the jogging shoes, stands, pulls off her dress exposing bright yellow running shorts and tank-top under. Places dress in bag.* WALTER *can't believe any of this altogether. He drops paper.*

WALTER. What the hell you doing!?

ELLIE. I jog every Monday, Wednesday and Friday. Will you watch my stuff for me, please? (*She trots off energetically*)

WALTER *stares off after her in amazement. He shakes his head, returns attention to paper. NATURE SOUNDS.*

MAN WITH THE PLASTIC SANDWICH

WALTER. (*Scanning, reading aloud, commenting aloud*) "Auto. Banker. Banking. Bank Trainee. (*He folds paper to another section*) "If I had a brother or sister who needed a job I would sincerely recommend that they call 555-0890." (*Lowers paper, looks blankly ahead*) If I had a brother or sister who needed a job I'd sincerely recommend that they commit suicide! (*Lifts paper, continues to read*) "Sales/Marketing—The man we are looking for will have at least three years experience, a B. A. in marketing. He will be a shirt-sleeve self starter who is willing to work long hours. He will have integrity and drive. He will interface with top management on all high-level marketing decisions. He will be willing to be away from his family for extended periods. He will be willing to sacrifice some weekends for field marketing projects. He will gladly accept a level entry salary of—(*Expression of disbelief*) twelve-thousand-dollars a year! (*Lowers paper, stares blankly ahead*) He will also be—Jesus Christ!

He whips glasses from face, returns them to jacket. He crumples paper, slams it to the ground angrily. He studies the discarded paper for a few seconds then rises, picks it up, places it in the trash basket. He returns to the bench, sits. He fidgets, looks about nervously, glances at his watch. ELLIE *trots into the scene briskly. She's winded. NATURE SOUNDS OUT.*

ELLIE. Hi!
WALTER. That was fast. Don't you get all sticky?
ELLIE. (*Flopping to bench*) I don't wear underwear.
WALTER. I had to ask.
ELLIE. Underwear's a drag. Terribly restrictive. Makes red marks—awful for the circulation. And it's much easier to go to the bathroom this way.

WALTER. Please — no details!

ELLIE. I haven't worn any since high school.

WALTER. You mean — you're into out of underwear.

ELLIE. It's as close as I can get to nudity from nine to five. I get out of everything right after work. I can't wait. As soon as I hit the apartment, everything goes. You wanna come to the nude beach with me this Sunday?

WALTER. Me? A nude beach? No way! I don't. I couldn't. I'd be too embarrassed.

ELLIE. You're not hung.

WALTER. Yeah, that's right, I'm not — wha — ? (*He can't believe it*)

ELLIE. It's all very matter of fact. Nobody looks.

WALTER. That's what they tell you. But out of the corners of their eyes they're all taking public snapshots.

ELLIE. (*Removing running shoes*) Nonsense. Say, did you happen to see that documentary on China last night? PBS.

WALTER. Alice only watches game shows.

ELLIE. I love public T. V. Julia Child is my very best favorite. She's cool. You should have seen her cut up a trout last week. It's awful about the baby seals, isn't it?

WALTER. Awful.

ELLIE. I like the news for the hard of hearing a lot, too. I turn off the sound and try to guess what they're saying. Do you know what this means? (*Does quick series of hand motions*)

WALTER. Sorry, I wasn't listening.

ELLIE. (*Going through hand motions*) It means — "I-think-you're-cute." (*Placing shoes in bag*) I ran into the most depressed guy sitting on the other side of the park.

WALTER. What the hell are you, a bench to bench therapist?

ELLIE. A few kind words never hurt, I say. He was an old dude who's wife died last month. He's out of touch. Lonely. I invited him over for spaghetti.
WALTER. I hope he's into nude cooking.
ELLIE. You know, Walter, old age is something.
WALTER. It's something alright.
ELLIE. We can't out run it, even in Adidas. I took care of one of my neighbors right up to the end. Nobody would have anything to do with her—not even her own children. People are afraid of old people. I think their funky. (*Digging bag of nuts and raisins from her bag*) Would you like some mixed nuts and raisins?
WALTER. No thanks.

They ruminate in silence, ELLIE *eats health mix.*

ELLIE. Ya know, I figure I save over a $100.00 a year.
WALTER. (*After a slow take*) On lunches?
ELLIE. On underwear.

Silence. ELLIE *shoves health mix at* WALTER, *he digs in. They sit chewing for a few seconds.*

ELLIE. I didn't mean to upset you awhile ago.
WALTER. Oh, that's okay. I over reacted. It's not every day I get an offer like that.
ELLIE. I was just trying to help.
WALTER. Thanks. I couldn't do a thing like that. I wouldn't be able to relax. The whole time I was making love to you I'd be seeing Alice's face. I haven't fooled around since we've been married. Over twenty years.
ELLIE. Faithfulness is nice.
WALTER. With you it could be for an hour.
ELLIE. So what? Who says there's a time limit!?
WALTER. Oh, I've thought about it—other women.

And the older I get the more I think about it—the pressure's building. My time's running out. I'd better do it before it's too late. But, when it comes down to it I can't go through with it—I get this mental block.

ELLIE. Alices face?

WALTER. Just like Mount Rushmore hanging over the whole thing.

ELLIE. Maybe you should force yourself. Once you got over the first hurdle maybe you'd be okay.

WALTER. It wouldn't work. I have an invisible shield of guilt around me. And Alice would know.

ELLIE. How?

WALTER. After twenty years a woman knows everything. A twitch, a blink, anything unusual is worth a million words. If I would have gone to your apartment Alice would know it the minute I hit the door—I would have mattress written all over me. She would know, her look would say it all. It would say, "you, you dirty sneaking rat, you met a beautiful, sexy young girl in the park and you took her to her apartment and ravaged her great joggers' body." Alice would know.

ELLIE. You really think so?

WALTER. I know so.

ELLIE. I mean, do you really think I'm good looking and sexy?

WALTER. Who said that?

ELLIE. You did, just now.

WALTER. I said that's what Alice would be thinking. (*Beat*) But, you are. You are good looking and sexy. Too damned sexy. Dangerous.

ELLIE. Then I attract you.

WALTER. Yeah. Yeah, you attract me.

ELLIE. That's the very first unbasic blue thing you've said today, you know that.

WALTER. I'm all heart.

ELLIE. And a very attractive guy.

WALTER. Well, I don't feel attractive. I feel like a great big pimple.

ELLIE. What about Alice, is it still the same, I mean, you know—good after all these years?

WALTER *reflects.*

WALTER. Yeah. You know, when she bends over to take something out of the oven I still get the twingies.

ELLIE. That's beautiful.

WALTER. Yeah.

ELLIE. Then, you still love her.

WALTER. Alice is a sweet, wonderful, decent person. When they made Alice there wasn't a mold, there was a grand design. It's too damned bad she's married to a big unemployed zit like me!

ELLIE. I really envy you.

WALTER. *You,* Envy *me*?

ELLIE. I have to envy anyone who's still in love after twenty years. And you're worried about being out of work? Hell, that's the least of your worries, you've got it made. Besides, something will turn up. I was out of work when I came to California. And now, now I'm on the way to paralegal. And I love it. Did you love Clinical whatever?

WALTER. Engineering. I guess. I dunno.

ELLIE. A person shouldn't do something he doesn't love. Is there anything you've always wanted to do? You know—like a hidden desire?

WALTER. I've always wanted to be a writer.

ELLIE. That's exciting! I love writers.

WALTER. I wrote good memos. You know, I never ever used the expression, "please be advised."

ELLIE. No! Not even once? Wow, that is creative! Edwards, Milliken, Stone and Katz would fold without, "please be advised."

WALTER. I also write a recap for our Christmas cards every year. I'd like to write a book—about my times growing up when I was a kid.

ELLIE. Do it—load it with sex, that way it will sell.

WALTER. Sex!? In my childhood? The most risque thing I ever did was feel-up a girl at a horror movie one time. She hit me with her Milk Duds! Anyway, it's too late now, I can't risk writing. I should have started when I was a kid, but my mother was against it. She said writers were irresponsible—that it was a dead end. She always told me, "think of you future, Walter. Don't wind up like your father. Get into something solid." My old man was a promoter, a dreamer, an idea man. I remember he used to sit on the back steps with a beer and stare off into space a lot. He had an idea for everything except how to pay the bills. If it wasn't for my mother doing odd jobs we would have been in big trouble. Some men were now and then between jobs, my dad was always between ideas. Once in awhile he'd stumble onto something and we'd have dough for a few days. He'd buy me and my mother all kinds of stuff, takes us on trips—the best hotels. While the money lasted, nothing was too good. But most of the time we spent hiding in the pantry so the bill collectors wouldn't know we were home. You have any idea what it's like hunching in a closet with your mom and dad? We used to play Parchesi by flashlight. So, I figured engineering was the way to go, that there'd always be a job for an engineer—right? So, I prepared, went to college, did all the numbers. The day I got the axe I couldn't believe it. And they didn't fire me, oh no! They, "phased me out!" I was phased out, just like an old model car. When they told me I was though I was mentally tranquilized. I couldn't talk, couldn't move even. I just sat there staring straight ahead getting sick to my stomach. Then I went to the men's room and threw up in the sink. Six years of college—(*Mimes, with finger in downward clockwise motion, "down the drain."*) At first I was so shook-up I couldn't leave the house. I kept my car in the garage so people would think I was still working. I sat in the den all day and drank Pepsis and watched the soaps—people with brain tumors and blindness and marital problems. It kept me going—next to their hang-ups unemployment was nothing.

ELLIE. Know what? You need a diversion. Tellya what—why don't you come backpacking Saturday. We're leaving early, eight of us. You can be my date.

WALTER. I'd crap out after one block.

ELLIE. Do you ever exercise?

WALTER. Well, I walk from the couch to the TV, from the TV to the refrigerator, from the refrigerator back to the couch.

ELLIE. You've got to keep in shape! (*Pulling him by the hand*) Here let me show you!

WALTER. (*Reluctant*) Forget it!

ELLIE. (*Tugging*) C'mon!

WALTER. Not here—in public!

ELLIE. (*Pulling him to his feet*) Don't be silly. On your feet!

WALTER. I'm not coordinated!

ELLIE. Nonsense! Now, c'mon. First—running in place! (*She begins to run in place effortlessly and gracefully*) C'mon—RUN!

WALTER. (*Begins to run, barely getting feet off of ground*) I feel like an idiot!

ELLIE. (*Running*) Isn't this fun!?

WALTER. (*Puffing*) Peachy!

ELLIE. (*Stops running*) Okay, now stretching! (*She reaches far overhead with both hands then swings down and touches her toes. Walter stands by watching, gasping.*) C'mon—STRETCH!

WALTER. (*Attempting exercise*) This is insane!

ELLIE. (*Demonstrating*) And—BEND!

WALTER. Crazy! (*Barely able to touch his knees*)

ELLIE. (*Looking great*) Isn't it easy!?

WALTER. Easy for you—I'm wearing underwear!

ELLIE. (*Stops stretching*) Now! Deep breathing! (*Throws arms wide apart, inhales deeply, collapses arms, exhales*) C'mon—try it!

WALTER. (*gasping, holding lower back*) I think I threw out my back.

ELLIE. BREATHE!

WALTER. (*Attempts exercise, lapses into a fit of coughing*) Forget it!

ELLIE. (*Stops deep breathing*) Now what!?

WALTER. (*Coughing, holding back, gasping*) It's bad enough breathing normally in this city!

ELLIE. You're just not used to it. After ten minutes a day you'll build up to it.

WALTER. After ten minutes a day I'll build up to a coronary.

ELLIE. Remember—every day!

WALTER. (*Collapsing on bench*) Sure, sure.

ELLIE. How about Saturday, then?

WALTER. I can't—Saturday's my day to clean the house.

ELLIE. What about Alice?

ELLIE, *under dialogue, exchanges jogging shoes for street shoes, slips into her dress, primps.*

MAN WITH THE PLASTIC SANDWICH 27

WALTER. Alice is selling real estate. She's doing it to help out.

ELLIE. That's great!

WALTER. I hate it! Especially if she'd be successful! I pray every day that she won't sell a house.

ELLIE. I don't get it.

WALTER. How the hell you think I'd feel if all of a sudden Alice became a member of the "Millionaire's Club!?" Next it would be Cadillacs and cigars — women go to any lengths these days! For years I've been the responsible provider, a guy who's been able to write checks with a flourish the tenth of every month. I brought home the bacon, I was in charge, I took care of Alice — I was SOMEBODY! I can't stand the thought of being an out-of-work bum and my wife a successful business woman! And I can't adjust to housework every Saturday! Dusting and cleaning and toilet bowls — being alone with Myron.

ELLIE. Myron?

WALTER. My brother-in-law.

ELLIE. A dead beat, huh?

WALTER. He's loaded. I wish to hell he was a flake, then I could take care of him. But the bastard's successful, everything he touches turns to assets. After his wife died he moved in with us.

ELLIE. Hit him up for a loan.

WALTER. I'm not stooping to borrowing from Myron. Myron's a self made man, and self made men never let you forget favors. It's bad enough living with his success story. If I've heard it once I've heard it a million times — "Myron only went as far as the eighth grade. Myron started out selling newspapers on a freezing street corner when he was only ten." I've never heard that he sold papers on warm, sunny days — it was always freezing! Like he only sold cold weather editions!!! If Pearl Harbor had been on July 7th no one in Myron's neighborhood would have known about World War II! My only answer is finding a job soon. Anything. I'll be a bus boy. Or maybe a parking lot attendant, I've always had an underlying destructive urge.

ELLIE. Look, I know it's got to be rough. You're going through a rotten period. But something will break. And anyway — you're rich! You've got Alice, someone who really cares, the most important thing. And nobody can "phase it out" after twenty years. And you're a sweet, decent person, Walter. A guy with morals. You're one in a million, take it from someone who knows. You're decent and honest and straight. The big three! Why, I'd trade in my shiny new typewriter for a guy like you anytime. (*Glances at her watch*) Wow! Look at the time! I gotta get back.

WALTER. Edwards, Milliken, Stone and Katz are waiting.

ELLIE. With open legal pads. So, hang in there, Walter. And write that book. I'll be looking for it.

WALTER. I'll load it with sex.

ELLIE. It can't miss!

WALTER. (*Extends hand*) Well, Ellie, see you 'round.

ELLIE *slips past his outstretched hand, kisses him on the cheek gently.*

ELLIE. See ya 'round, basic blue. And, watch those steroids!

NATURE SOUNDS. ELLIE, *bag in hand, turns and exits briskly.* WALTER *stands for a moment, looking off after her. He turns, spots his half eaten sandwich on the bench. He retrieves the sandwich, spoon, yogurt cup, tosses them into the trash container. He walks CENTER, raises hands overhead, stretches, drops arms.*

WALTER. Nuts!

END ACT ONE

ACT TWO

Two months later. NATURE SOUNDS. WALTER, *in shirt sleeves, does a quick series of stretches, jogs about clumsily, becomes quickly enervated due to this feeble attempt at exercise. He takes neatly folded jacket from bench, dons it. His attire is the same as in Act One save one glaringly evident sartorial touch: a bright yellow necktie.* WALTER *seats himself next to his opened attache. A profusion of official looking papers, a litter of brochures are evident both in case and on bench.* WALTER *draws half-glasses from jacket pocket, places them carefully on tip of nose, lifts brochure, studies it. He takes sandwich from case, absentmindedly munches at it while perusing material. He flips brochure aside, returns glasses to jacket, stands. He adjusts himself, straightens his tie. He raps on back of bench with a stiff, professional air. He launches into his sales pitch: NATURE SOUNDS OUT.*

WALTER. Oh, hello there—Mrs. Robert Martin? I'm Walter Price of California Hot Tibs—I mean—Hot Tubs, dammit! (*He "knocks" again*) Hello, Mrs. Martin? My name is Walter Tubs. Dammit to hell!!!!! I can't even get my own name right! (*"Knocks" again, clears throat*) Good Morning, Mrs. Martin, I'm Walter Price of California Hot Tubs and I've come in answer to your inquiry and . . . and . . . and—ah hell! There's no

MAN WITH THE PLASTIC SANDWICH 31

flow. It's not a grabber. My pitch stinks! I'll never make a salesman.

WALTER *removes the munched sandwich from bench, folds foil around it, takes it to the trash container and prepares to drop it inside. His actions are thwarted by a VOICE OFF STAGE.*

HALEY. Hey, hey—don't throw that away!

WALTER *starts. HALEY FISK ENTERS briskly snatches the wrapped sandwich from WALTER'S hand.*

HALEY. Never discard a morsel, my good man, not when people are going hungry in this world!

WALTER, *stunned, watches as* HALEY *moves to bench with sandwich.* HALEY *seats himself on bench.* HALEY *is sixty five years old and it's immediately discernable that he is a soldier of the road. He's a distinguished looking man with strong features and, even though scruffy, bears the indelible stamp of class. He's wearing an old tweed sports jacket, slightly tattered. His slacks are cheap tan twill but have a definite flair. His shirt is an ancient classic; a well faded pink button-down. He's sporting a colorful bandana at his neck. His shoes are of the work variety, but shined.* HALEY *is tattered elegant.* WALTER *watches* HALEY *with stunned disbelief as he meticulously goes about ritual of preparing to dine.* HALEY *withdraws another bandana from jacket pocket, spreads it across his legs. Then he pulls a knife, fork, spoon, a salt and pep-*

per from other jacket pocket, places these items on bench seat. HALEY *carefully unwraps the foil, peers in at contents.* WALTER *advances upon* HALEY *cautiously.*

HALEY. Ah ha! Peanut butter and jelly!
WALTER. (*Moving in*) No steroids.
HALEY. Yes, and totally boneless. The fillet of sandwiches. And a quick energy booster as well. (*He bites into sandwich with gusto*)
WALTER. You're actually going to eat that?
HALEY. Witness! (*Holding sandwich aloft*) I *am* eating it!
WALTER. Other people's food, just like that?
HALEY. Would you eat something that was tainted?
WALTER. Of course not!
HALEY. Well—in that case. (*Another bite*)
WALTER. I couldn't do that, not in a million years. I'd be scared to death of picking up something. I have a low tolerance to germs. And I'm a finicky eater.
HALEY. Too bad. (*Munching with delight*)
WALTER. In restaurants I always wipe off my silver with my napkin before I eat.
HALEY. Bad manners.
WALTER. I don't trust those commercial dish washers. And if there's a crack in my cup or plate—back it goes. It comes from my childhood, the way I was brought up. My mother always used section plates so stuff wouldn't run together.
HALEY. It all winds up in the same place, a mixture of glop to be digested by the human juices.
WALTER. A beautiful thought.
HALEY. (*Munching*) A little heavy on the jelly, don't you think?

WALTER. You grab food out of the trash, now you're complaining?

HALEY. Just an observation. The ratio of peanut butter to the jelly is the key to the preparation of this delectible edible.

WALTER. When I made it I didn't think I was going to be graded on it!

HALEY. In cooking it's the nuances that count.

WALTER. The next time I make meat loaf I'll try to remember to keep my calculator handy.

HALEY. Meat loaf's a tough dish to prepare. I never look down my nose at meat loaf.

WALTER. No—you look down a trash basket at it. Tell me—how the hell can you grab up food from a total stranger?

HALEY. I think hunger has a lot to do with it. And you looked like the kind of man a person could eat after.

WALTER. Thanks . . . I think.

HALEY. You're a meticulous person, I could tell that by the way you dress. Are you a floor walker?

WALTER. (*Seating himself on bench*) No!

HALEY. I've go it—a hotel clerk.

WALTER. It's none of your business.

HALEY. Ah ha—life insurance, right!?

WALTER. Ah ha—life insurance, WRONG!? (*Brief silence, Walter looks at paper*)

HALEY. Undertaker?

WALTER. Sorry.

HALEY. Well, you should be, you have the perfect casketside manner. You know, undertaking's an honorable profession, an important function. Somebody has to do it.

WALTER. What the hell is this? Sociology One?

Silence as WALTER *watches* HALEY *return silver-*

ware, bandana, salt & peppers to jacket pocket. Meticulous operation. HALEY *pulls handfull of cigar butts from pocket.*

HALEY. (*Offering Walter a butt*) Cigar?
WALTER. I don't smoke.
HALEY. Finest tobacco. (*Running butt under nose*) And—presmoked!
WALTER. Also prelipped!
HALEY. From behind the L. A. Country Club— nothing but the best.
WALTER. Look—If you don't mind, I have some work to do. Okay? (*Brief silence, Haley lights up, puffs*)
HALEY. I know—cemetary lots!!!
WALTER. What the hell is this with cemetery lots!? Do I smell like embalming fluid or something? Look—do me a favor, friend—
HALEY. Haley. Haley Fisk. (*Pulls card from jacket artfully*) My card.
WALTER. (*Takes card, tosses it aside*) Please—would you mind leaving me alone.
HALEY. You're a very irritable person, you know that?
WALTER. Look, it's not everyday that I get food grabbed out of my hands by an Ivy League derelict.
HALEY. What makes you say Ivy League?
WALTER. Because you look like you do your shopping at a Goodwill in New Haven.
HALEY. You're a very perceptive fellow under your irascible facade.
WALTER. Is there anything at all that I can do to insult you into philosophizing at another bench.
HALEY. I don't insult easily.
WALTER. I've got that figured out.

MAN WITH THE PLASTIC SANDWICH 35

HALEY. (*Indicating with cigar at the papers*) What's this mass of institutional looking crap?

WALTER. None of your business!

HALEY. Thank God for that.

WALTER. It's sales information.

HALEY. (*Puffing away*) Ah yes—executive toilet paper.

WALTER. Why am I talking to you? Why?

HALEY. It's pap, a blight upon our land. A sad testimonial to our time.

WALTER. Maybe I should have been an undertaker. That way you don't get conversation.

HALEY. The last time the world was destroyed by water. The next time—PAPER! We'll all drown in a rising sea of handbills, stuffers, paper boxes and bags. All humanity will fall victim to a tidal wave of pulp.

WALTER. Are you sure that's a cigar you're smoking?

HALEY. Mark my word—mankind will be inundated.

WALTER. What is it about me that always attracts nuts? Why can't I go off somewhere and be alone like other people? (*Pointing off*) See that guy over there? He's been here everyday I have and no one ever stops to bother him, no one grabs his left overs, no one gives a dirty damn what kind of underwear he's wearing! What is it with me? Am I some kind of freak, or something?

HALEY. You have a very definite moral and frustrated quality; the look of a man who's just learned his daughter's been ravaged by a motorcycle gang.

WALTER. I don't have a daughter.

HALEY. It's rough on a moral person in this immoral world. That's one of the big reasons you're frustrated.

WALTER. You don't know anything about me!

HALEY. You're life's an open attache case.

WALTER. You have all the answers, don't you?

HALEY. Not all — but I'm close.

WALTER. Maybe you'll have 'em by Friday. So, why don't you meet me here next week and fill me in?

HALEY. Your entire aura spells — *anxiety*! You're a very tight person, I can tell.

WALTER. You mean by the way my peanut butter and jelly was squeezed together? I know! You're a fortune teller! You read garbage!!!!!

HALEY. You're just another victim of All American Tension. You're being stretched on the rack of society. (*Points finger quickly at Walter's legs*) Look at that!!!!!

WALTER. Look at what!?

HALEY. The muscles in your legs are like piano wires, I can see them twitching through your pants. We had a fellow like that in our office. Tension began creeping in subtley. First, a slight jerk at the side of his mouth, then a more pronounced twitch in his neck.

WALTER. If he worked around you much I can understand.

HALEY. He was me!

WALTER. You?

HALEY. I became riddled with ticks. My entire body was a symphony of twitches. And my blood pressure went through the roof. And then, the bleeding ulcer.

WALTER. I hope this is the *bad* news.

HALEY. At forty five my mind and body were going.

WALTER. How old are you?

HALEY. I'll be sixty-five in April.

WALTER. What!? You look younger than I do!

HALEY. Frustration!

WALTER. I dunno, I've always looked old, even as a baby. I couldn't have been frustrated then.

HALEY. It can begin in the womb.

WALTER. Pre-natal tension?

HALEY. It's a new theory.

WALTER. There's a new theory for everything; a new religion; a new wacko cure, some stupid fad diet. Last month my wife, Alice, went on a cottage cheese diet—nothing but cottage cheese morning, noon and night. She lost eighteen pounds but her breath—*oh*! I don't buy the pre-natal business. Age is just me, that's all. I looked like a senior all through grade school. And I could get a drink when I was thirteen. Most kids carried an I. D.—I carried a face.

HALEY. I'm not talking about your face, I'm talking about your legs. (*Pointing quickly*) There! See it!?

WALTER. See what!?

HALEY. A twitch!

WALTER. I don't feel any twitch.

HALEY. That's the pity of it. It's become habit, it's taking over. You're no longer in control.

WALTER. You're crazy!

HALEY. Watch and see, if you don't believe me.

WALTER. I'm not sitting around staring at my legs.

HALEY. (*Staring at Walters legs, close proximity*) Shhhhhhhhh! Quiet! Just watch. (*They silently watch Walter's legs intently*)

WALTER. (*Breaking a long silence*) I feel like I'm fishing!

HALEY. Shhhhhhh! (*Long silence*)

WALTER. You want me to pull up my trousers?

HALEY. No, it'll be easier to spot it this way—when your pants rustle. Now silence! (*Silence*) There! See it!!!???

WALTER. Yeah.

HALEY. Uncontrollable tension.

WALTER. Jesus! I'm a walking pants full of piano wires.

HALEY. Stand up, stretch a bit. It'll relieve the spasms.

WALTER. Do you have a degree in tension? (*Standing, begins to run in place*)

HALEY. I have, my good man, a degree in life. I'm a free spirit.

WALTER. (*Running*) Sure, sure, I know the bit—you've got it made.

HALEY. I have, my good man—ah Mr.?

WALTER. Walter. Walter Price.

HALEY. I have, my good Walter, got it by the proverbial ass.

WALTER. Second hand stogies and used food is by the ass? Don't play Charlie Chaplin with me—most tramps are miserable. (*Panting, starting to stretch—touch toes*)

HALEY. That's because most never have a choice. With me it was self-imposed exile.

WALTER. From what, prison? (*Attempting to touch toes*)

HALEY. (*Withdrawing another card from jacket*) Have another card.(*Walter stops stretching, takes card*)

WALTER. (*Studies card for second, holding away*) You!? A Vice President?

HALEY. Why not? Everybody else was.

WALTER. (*At card*) And General Manager? C'mon.

HALEY. I was G. M., Commander In Chief, Head Honcho, Top Dog.

WALTER. Well—arf arf to you! Once top dog, now a common curr, right?

HALEY. Quite wrong.

WALTER. With B. R. M. & O.!? They're the biggest!

HALEY. The biggest, the bestest, and the most resplendent with glorious bullshit! And they hand out the greatest twitches on Madison Avenue.

WALTER. C'mon—you stole this.

HALEY. I only steal food. No, it's the bitter truth. I keep the cards as a constant reminder, so that I'll never forget my pressurized journey down ulcer alley.

WALTER. You mean, you actually—

HALEY. I actually, really, legitimately ran one of the largest advertising agencies in the world. I ran an empire, a dynasty, a billion-dollar-baby. I was, Walter my lad, referred to in the biz as . . . "Mr. Gray Flannel." I had a salary that read like a telephone number, I received a bonus that would choke a giraffe, and my expense account just wasn't unlimited—it was obscene. I had a company car with a company chauffeur, a company dining room with a company chef, a company psychiatrist with a company couch. I, Walter, was—A COMPANY MAN!

WALTER. (*Looking at card*) Haley Fisk. The name *is* vaguely familiar.

HALEY. You probably saw it in Newsweek, Time, Esquire, Forbes or Fortune. I made them all—you name it. I was the wunderkind of copy, the brainchild of snappy jingles. Believe it or not, this somewhat tattered knight once spearheaded some of the biggest projects ever. Remember the Wilson Wax campaign?

WALTER. (*Thinking*) "The Glaze of Wine and Roses?"

HALEY. That was me.

WALTER. No!

HALEY. Every trite and pithy line. I thought up the slogan over six martinis at 21. Remember—"We Don't Fly Planes, We Fly People?"

WALTER. Trans-National Airlines!

HALEY. Right. How about—"When Seconds Count, You Can Count On Us?"

40 MAN WITH THE PLASTIC SANDWICH

WALTER. That was Federated Casualty. The guy in the sincere suit with the steel gray head.

HALEY. Remember the American Dairy Co-op slogan?

WALTER. I think so. "We Pull Together!" (*Mimes milking*)

HALEY. You may not know tension but you know your commercials.

WALTER. You really did all those?

HALEY. I confess, I'm the guilty party. I did dozens. The copy, the works.

WALTER. I remember reading about you once in the Wall Street Journal. Haley Fisk, yeah! You're the guy who put the Rib-It Barbeque chain on the map.

HALEY. (*Reflecting*) "Even the frogs say Rib-It."

WALTER. The guy dressed up in the frog suit.

HALEY. That was it. Do you remember the jingle?

WALTER. Sure!

HALEY. Ready!?

WALTER. Why not?

HALEY. (*Counts off 3/4 time*) One, two, three—one, two, three. (*They sing in unison to the tune of, "East Side West Side,"—Haley does a time step.*)
Rib-It, Rib-It
The ribs so pure and true,
Tasty, wholesome
King of the barbeque
Rib-It, Rib-It
The ribs that are so spare
Made in our country kitchens,
(*last line in rubato and harmony*)
With—tender—lov—ing—care.

HALEY. Very good! Maybe we should take it on the road.

WALTER. It was Alice's favorite commercial. Man, you had it made. Now all you've got is someone else's cigar.

HALEY. (*puffs*) And a noble root, I must say. Yes, Walter my boy, but now I've got my sanity, peace of mind. All I had before was a romance with imported gin.

WALTER. Straight up or on the rocks?

HALEY. My blood pressure was straight up and my marriage was on the rocks. It was my third marriage to my third socialite. She was straight out of Town & Country—cashmere sweaters over button-down shirts and a full time frost over her heart. She possessed all the warmth of a collection agent. Beautiful—but no feeling.

WALTER. I went with a girl like that once. Her eyes were just like a goldfish's—no expression.

HALEY. Her name was Bunny.

WALTER. Bunny. Why do uppercrusters have names like that? You know—Bunny, Petey, Binkey?

HALEY. Because people with money work at being exclusive. It's all they have to do, this strange little cult of idle trust funders.

WALTER. Your family had money?

HALEY. Old money.

WALTER. Old—new—who cares? It's one of the few things that wrinkles don't make ugly.

HALEY. Who needs it?

WALTER. I needs it.

HALEY. It's a great green millstone.

WALTER. It gives you mobility.

HALEY. I have total mobility. (*Begins to pace, circling the bench, speaking dramatically like an Elizabethan actor*) Two weeks ago I was frolicking in the rarified atmosphere of mile-high Denver. Last week I was strolling the sun washed streets of San Francisco, inhaling the succulent odors of the steaming sea food that were wafting their way toward me from the nearby wharf. (*Rambling on dramatically*) Tonight I'll be in Palm Springs. Palm Springs, Walter, an oasis for the Gods. I'll be languishing under an undulating date palm, drinking in the serenity of the desert night. (*Inhales deeply*) Ah—that air! Let me ask you—just how far have your adventures taken you during the past week?

WALTER. Over a thousand miles!

HALEY. Really? Not bad.

WALTER. Yeah—but all in L. A.

HALEY. Ah then, who has the mobility!? Money, my boy, buys material. And material piles up and propagates. And one day you wake up the overseer of a rabbit plantation. You wind up with—ITEMS! After my second marriage it took six months to divide the ITEMS! The teak, the china, the signed pieces. Remember—money buys items, objects 'd art, heirlooms.

WALTER. Well, at our house it pays insurance premiums.

HALEY. Insurance! Another boil on the butt of society! There is no such thing as insurance. The idea is to own nothing—that way you have nothing to loose! The only thing that counts is living to the fullest every single, wonderful day! Life is beautiful, Walter—just like a great big peanut butter and jelly sandwich oozing with excitement and adventure. But most people are afraid to take a bite out of it, to sink their teeth into it! Instead they waste their days chewing away on a flavorless, routine existence. Poor devils—their sandwich is plastic!

WALTER. Alluva sudden I feel like I'm audience for some kind of crazy road show.

HALEY. Quite right! I am a road show, traveling the circus of life. My tent is on my back, my wits are my performers and they're treading the high wire without a net.

WALTER. Yeah, and while you're out treading the high wire other people are treading the pavement.

HALEY. You think I don't work?

WALTER. Let's just say I don't think you're buying too many lunches.

HALEY. Don't insult my dignity, sir. I do the work of the world—what ever pleases me. I do what I have to do whenever I have to do it! Until I generate enough, just enough mind you, enough income to enable me to press on toward new horizons, new faces, new adventures! In the clothing that you see now I function in the capacity of loveable domestic—house man, cook, chauffeur. (*Removing jacket*) This, Walter, is my outer shell, the garb that projects the sophisticated, Haley Fisk. (*Tossing jacket over back of bench*) My most recent pleasure was instructing a cook in a Bel Air household regarding the finer points of Chinese cuisine. (*Unbuttoning shirt*) A most delicate art, the preparation of Oriental dishes. (*Pulling off shirt revealing a work shirt underneath*) I developed culinary dexterity, among many other talents, while traveling this great land. (*Tosses shirt over back of park bench, begins to unzip his trousers*).

WALTER. What the hell you doing!?

HALEY. I'm removing the grand drape that obscures another reality, another dimension.

WALTER. This isn't a road show, this is a striptease!

HALEY. (*Starting to remove his pants, revealing a pair of well worn jeans underneath*) Yes! And the hand is quicker than the eye. Every little movement has a meaning all its own! Chameleon like I'm peeling away the facade of classic drifter and revealing the tarnished, but noble hide of . . . (*Whipping off outer trousers with elan, underscoring the next line*) Haley Fisk— TRADESMAN! (*He stands at attention and salutes. Walter sits stunned for a moment. Then, he begins to applaud. Haley bows elegantly*)

WALTER. Amazing! Two layers.

HALEY. The complete and functional wardrobe. Now, bring on the painting, the plumbing, the wallpaper, the carpentry. I'm ready!

WALTER. You can do all that?

HALEY. With ease an proficiency.

WALTER. I've never been any good at things like that, I have no facility for it. When I paint it always runs down the brush onto my hand and down my arm off my elbow onto my pants. I can't even roller coat. I always splatter. I get little speckles all over everything. In my family they called people like you "handy." Well, I'm not handy. I have trouble even getting toilet paper on the roll—that little round thing keeps springing out on me.

HALEY. No one can be that inept.

WALTER. You have no idea. I even have trouble unscrewing light bulbs.

HALEY. They unscrew to the left.

WALTER. Not for me they don't.

HALEY. They do for everybody. It's international.

WALTER. I can only get my fingers to screw to the right. And I never know when they're cool enough.

HALEY. Your fingers?

WALTER. Yes. No! The light bulbs. I always unscrew them while they're still blazing hot and they fry my hand.

HALEY. You appear to be an intelligent man. A bit lack-luster, perhaps, but intelligent. What's you profession, Walter?

WALTER. Do you know about Clinical Engineering?

HALEY. Spare me. I abhor the word—"clinical." It says so much.

WALTER. Well, anyway, I'm heavy into clinical. Or I was, that is, for over twenty years.

HALEY. That explains the lack luster. (*Gestures across mass of papers*) Then, I assume, this abundance of intimidating tripe represents—engineering.

WALTER. No—it represents hot tubs.

HALEY. I usually perceive readily, but in this case—

WALTER. I was a Clinical Engineer for years. Then I was canned. Bang! Just like that.

HALEY. Ah yes—the big bang theory.

WALTER. And I was out of work for six months. I couldn't find a damn thing. Then I saw an ad for a hot tubs salesman I jumped at it.

HALEY. I hate to confess ignorance but what, pray tell, are—hot tubs?

WALTER. They're a California craze.

HALEY. Everything's a craze in California.

WALTER. They're large—(*Grabbing brochure from case, shoving it into Haley's hands*) Here. They're large, redwood tubs that you install in your house, your yard, sun deck—like that. You fill them with warm water and sit in them. (*Haley sitting on bench, studying brochure*) They're very relaxing, very therapeutic.

HALEY. Frankly, I'm repulsed.

WALTER. So am I. That's probably the reason I'm having trouble selling the damn things.

HALEY. Are they expensive?

WALTER. They don't give them away.

HALEY. How many have you sold? (*Into brochure*)

WALTER. One lousy tub! The commission didn't even cover my draw. Then the tub was defective and they sent me out to troubleshoot. When I got there the entire family was sitting in the thing stark naked! I couldn't take the sight of all that skin at one time. Nine people sitting there nude—I couldn't look at them while we talked. If they'd just been wearing something—eye patches even. Garters.

HALEY. (*Into brochure*) I sense a great potential here.

WALTER. Really?

HALEY. Take it from a former marketing wizard, Walter, tubs are going to be big.

WALTER. You think?

HALEY. How does one obtain his contacts?

WALTER. The company runs ads in the paper and when people write in they send their inquiries to me.

HALEY. Cold lead selling.

WALTER. Jesus, do you know everything? Amazing. Before you showed up I was practicing my sales pitch.

HALEY. Let me hear it.

WALTER. What?

HALEY. Your pitch.

WALTER. I'd be too embarrassed.

HALEY. If you're embarrassed, how can you sell? C'mon, you've got to sharpen the tools of your trade.

WALTER. Are you serious?

HALEY. Certainly.

WALTER. I can't. I'll blush.

HALEY. (*Standing.*) Nonsense. Now c'mon, sell me. But fair warning—I'm not going to be easy.

WALTER. Well . . . okay.

WALTER *adjusts his jacket, straightens his tie, clears throat. Many gyrations of long duration.*

HALEY. What in heaven's name are you doing?
WALTER. I'm getting ready.
HALEY. Don't be so formal, you're not opening at the Met.
WALTER. Okay, now I'll knock on the back of the bench. That'll be the front door.
HALEY. Alright, alright — get on with it!

WALTER *clears his throat, raps on the back of the bench.*

HALEY. (*Pantomiming opening door*) Yes?
WALTER. (*Stiff, nervous*) Good afternoon, Mr. Fisk —
HALEY. Sorry, Mr. Fisk isn't here!
WALTER. My name is Walter Price and I'm with California Hot — Wha? What the? How the hell am I going to sell if you're not here?
HALEY. I'm faking it. I'm really home but I'm circumventing solicitors.
WALTER. This is ridiculous!
HALEY. I'm merely exercising a common ploy.
WALTER. How am I supposed to sharpen my tools if I don't have anything to sharpen them on? This is playlike! Remember!?
HALEY. It's a real obstacle that you're going to face time and again. And you've got to be prepared to overcome it. You've just driven fifty miles on a hot, smoggy day to follow up a lead. You've arrived at your destination and the prospect isn't on the premises. Now what?

WALTER. I get sick on his welcome mat.

HALEY. No — you exhaust every possibility. You ask if the lady of the house is in. If not, you ask for a responsible member of the household. Alright?

WALTER. Alright.

HALEY. Well, go ahead — ask! Just don't stand there on my doorstep with your brochure hanging out! Speak up man!

WALTER. Okay okay! (*Clears throat*) May I see, Mrs. Fisk, please?

HALEY. Sorry, she's out of town.

WALTER. Then, could I talk with another member of the family?

HALEY. They're all in St. Louis.

WALTER. (*slamming brochure to the ground*) What the hell you think you're doing!!!!!?????

HALEY. I'm putting you off.

WALTER. No — you're PISSING ME OFF!!!!! I should have known better than to get into this with you. Why won't I ever learn!?

HALEY. I'm presenting a typical problem situation. How do you solve it?

WALTER. By punching the prospect in the mouth!!!!!

HALEY. You solve it by intriguing him.

WALTER. Do I wink or show him some leg?

HALEY. You stimulate his appetite. Like this — listen: "I'm terribly sorry no one's home. (*Extending his hand to Walter who takes it*) The name's Price, Walter Price. California Hot Tubs. I've driven out in response to an inquiry. It's unfortunate that the Fisk's aren't around because we're offering a special discount, for a limited time, on our top-of-the-line tub. By the way, you happen to know the date, sir. The fifteenth? Oh my, isn't that luck for you. The offer expires today. Well, that's the way it goes. Here's my card. Would you be good

WALTER. How'd you guess!!!!!?????
HALEY. Well then, get the hell out before you start hating yourself!

BLACKOUT.

END ACT TWO

ACT THREE

Three weeks later. NATURE SOUNDS. WALTER is bespectacled in half-glasses. He is intent upon writing upon a legal tablet which he is holding in his lap. He's wearing a mad-plaid sports jacket, the bright yellow necktie. After a brief stint of writing he puts the legal pad aside, pen inside jacket. He withdraws the classified section of newspaper from case, begins to peruse. Suddenly, LENORE bursts onto the scene. She is a woman between thirty and thirty five years of age. She has a devastating body and is clad in a dress that traces her every curve and crevice. Her makeup is heavy, her hair style extreme. She's carrying an oversize shoulder bag. Her bigger-than-life quality is exaggerated by a pair of super-high platform shoes. LENORE is quite obviously harried, is breathless, obviously pressed. She races straight to WALTER who is still locked in concentration over the newspaper. She plops herself down next to WALTER causing him to react with a start, whip off glasses. NATURE SOUNDS OUT.

LENORE. (*Grabbing him by the sleeves*) Act like you know me!
WALTER. Huh!? (*Dropping paper*)
LENORE. Someone's after me!
WALTER. Who? What!? (*Slips glasses into jacket*)
LENORE. Behind you! Don't look around! Don't look!

enough to give it to the Fisk's when they return? Thank you. Good day, sir!" You turn and begin to walk away.

WALTER. That's the easy part.

HALEY. If the man's interested he'll never let you get to the end of his walkway.

WALTER. But that way he'd have to admit that he was home. That he lied.

HALEY. That's the buyer's perrogative.

WALTER. But there's no discount!

HALEY. There's *always* a discount! On a top-of-the-line tub you can afford to take it off the top of your commission.

WALTER. (*Slumping to bench*) I'll never make it, I'm just not a salesman.

HALEY. Can the negativity. Of course you'll be a salesman. Think positive, my boy. Now, Walter, once more. Into the breech!

WALTER. Forget it.

HALEY. C'mon!

WALTER. I'll never get it.

HALEY. I've never lost a pupil yet. On your feet, student!

WALTER. (*Rising*) If you insist.

HALEY. Go ahead—knock.

WALTER. (*Pulling himself together*) Okay. (*He knocks*)

HALEY. (*Opening "door"*) Yes?

WALTER. Good afternoon—Mr. Fisk?

HALEY. At your service.

WALTER. (*Extending his hand*) My name is Walter Tubs of California Hot Price.

HALEY. (*Taking Walter's hand, shaking it briskly*) Oh yes, we've been expecting you. (*Shouting off over shoulder*) Marge! California Hot Tubs!

WALTER. Marge?

HALEY. The wife.

WALTER. Oh yes—the wife. Well, Mr. Fisk, in answer to your inquiry, I've got just the tub for you.

HALEY. Good!

WALTER. Twelve thousand gallons, five feet deep with a capacity of eight people.

HALEY. It sounds perfect.

WALTER. (*Thinking*) Or is it, eighty thousand gallons, eight feet deep for five people?

HALEY. That sounds good, too.

WALTER. Or is it, fifty five thousand gallons? No—I think it's eighty five. Now, wait a minute—

HALEY. It sounds great, whatever. What's the price?

WALTER. For only thirty five hundred. (*Stops*) For only thirty three hundred. (*Stops*) For fifty three—(*Halts, then blurts onward*) For just forty four hundred dollars we can put you and your family in this beautiful five gallon, seven person—fifty five thousand, eight person, twenty foot deep tub. You can dive in it.

HALEY. Walter.

WALTER. (*Rolling*) We can put you and Marge and the kids in—

HALEY. Walter!

WALTER. (*Out of control*) Into this seventeen gallon, eight foot deep, solid oak, solid redwood. This solid redwood hot tub can be yours for just—

HALEY. Walter!

WALTER. For only—

HALEY. Walter!

WALTER. Thirty five hundred—

HALEY. Walter!

WALTER. Fifty three hundred—

HALEY. Walter! WALTER! You hate selling hot tubs, don't you?

MAN WITH THE PLASTIC SANDWICH 53

WALTER. (*Instinctively begins to turn head*) Where!?
LENORE. Don't look! (*Jerking him*) Keep looking at me!
WALTER. What the hell is this!?
LENORE. I'm in big trouble. Act like you're talking.
WALTER. I am, I'm talking.
LENORE. I mean, *really* talking.
WALTER. Okay, I'm *really* talking.

WALTER *begins to turn away*.

LENORE. Keep looking at me!
WALTER. (*Starts to rise*) Forget it! See you 'round!
LENORE. (*Desperate, pulling him down*) Please! Help me!
WALTER. I don't need involvements!
LENORE. All I'm asking is that you fake it for a few minutes. Please—go along!
WALTER. This damned park!

LENORE. Act like you're mad at me!
WALTER. I don't have to act! I hate you, I can't stand you! I don't know you—but you're a jerk! A wacko!
LENORE. Great! Keep it up! Now—slap me!
WALTER. *What*!!!???
LENORE. In the face—quick!
WALTER. I'm tempted. But forget it!
LENORE. (*Pointing at cheek*) Right here. A quickie!
WALTER. I'm not slugging a total stranger.
LENORE. Please—go for my jaw!
WALTER. I'm going for a cop! (*Rising*)
LENORE. Oh no—please, don't do that! C'mon, just a quick slap!
WALTER. Why should I? What's this all about?

LENORE. I'll explain later.

WALTER. Explain it to the squirrels, I'm leaving! (*Attempting to leave*)

LENORE. (*Holding his jacket*) Please! (*Note of desperation*) Don't leave me here alone, mister! (*Holding her hand near her face*) Here, slap my hand.

WALTER. Your hand!?

LENORE. It'll look like a slap.

WALTER. No!

LENORE. I'm desperate!

WALTER. It's that bad?

LENORE. You have no idea! Please, c'mon.

WALTER. I've got to be out of my mind for doing this! (*He smacks her palm, she reacts with mock pain*)

LENORE. Great! Again!

WALTER. Crazy, that's what I am! (*He fakes another blow, she reels, mock sobbing*)

LENORE. Now, I'm going to call you an awful name! Then, you hit me again!

WALTER. This can't be happening to Walter Price!

LENORE. YOU SONOFABITCH!

WALTER. Insane, that's what! (*He gives her another "slap." She reacts.*)

LENORE. Now, call me a bitch.

WALTER. With pleasure.

LENORE. Hurry!

WALTER. YOU BITCH!

LENORE. Now, make it dirty bitch!

WALTER. YOU DIRTY BITCH!

LENORE. Great! (*Withdrawing man's wristwatch from her bag*) Here, take this!

WALTER. (*Staring at watch*) What's this!?

LENORE. A watch. Put it in your pocket, quick!

WALTER. You're a pickpocket, that's what. A thief! I'm calling the police!

LENORE. If you leave he'll beat me for sure. Just a few more minutes, that's all I ask. PLEASE! (*She stands*)

WALTER. (*Shoving watch into his pocket*) I know I'm going to regret this.

LENORE. Now, pull me onto the bench. Make it rough!

WALTER, Walter Price, aiding a criminal. (*He pulls her to bench roughly. Lenore sits and looks off around Walter*) Well—what's he doing?

LENORE. It worked! He's leaving!

WALTER. (*Grabbing case*) Good, so am I. I'll look for your mug shots!

LENORE. Hey, wait a minute, come back here!

WALTER. (*Leaving*) Goodbye!!!!!

LENORE. You've GOT MY WATCH!

WALTER. (*Halting, feeling pocket*) Oh my God! You're right. I almost walked off with a pocket full of hot evidence. (*Removing watch, returning to Lenore on bench*) Here—be my guest.

LENORE. (*She stands, takes watch, plants a solid kiss on Walter's cheek*) My hero!

WALTER. What the hell's that for?

LENORE. For being nice.

WALTER. I'm not nice—I'm crazy.

LENORE. You're a real ace. Most guys would run out.

WALTER. That's because most guys have good sense. But not me, oh no, not me—I went through with it like some idiot. Standing up for some looney! Why, why me!?

LENORE. Because you're a gentleman.

WALTER. I know. I'm old school. And old school's old hat. I'm doomed in this day and age. I'm a door opener. I say thank you. And I still tip my hat and I don't even wear a hat anymore. (*Miming hat tip*) I do this.

LENORE. That's nice.

WALTER. It's stupid! My manners get me into big trouble. And this damned bench—it's jinxed!

LENORE. How can a bench be jinxed?

WALTER. Everytime I sit here I meet nutsies! Why won't people let me alone?

LENORE. Because you look like an okay guy.

WALTER. I'm sick of okay. It's a flaw in my personality. I'm just a soft touch, dammit. I can't say no. I've got, "Mr. Easy," written all over me. (LENORE *sits, opens purse, withdraws compact, begins to apply makeup*) Panhandlers cross the street to hit me for spare change. At Christmas Salvation Army people always ring their bells a little louder when I pass by. I try to be repulsive, but I can't pull it off.

LENORE. You repulsive? Forget it.

WALTER. I have a face that magnetizes problems, strangies. Like today. I come here to do a little writing and I wind up slapping a jewel thief.

LENORE. (*Primping*) I'm not a jewel thief, honey.

WALTER. Don't tell me watch repair.

LENORE. (*Returning compact to bag*) I'm a prostitute.

WALTER. What!? You—a woman of the night!? (*Slumps to bench*)

LENORE. Of the night, of the morning, the afternoon. You name it. My time is your time.

WALTER. Don't say *my* time.

LENORE. You've never paid for it?

WALTER. No, I've never paid for it! You actually are. I mean, a real honest to goodness—

LENORE. Hooker.

WALTER. Wow!

LENORE. You're staring at me.

WALTER. I'm sorry. It's just that I've never seen one up close before.

LENORE. You wanna touch me?
WALTER. No no.
LENORE. Go ahead. I feel just like people.
WALTER. You already kissed me.
LENORE. Has anything fallen off?
WALTER. If Alice ever found out that I was kissed by a—a—
LENORE. Hooker. It's easy to say. Nothing to it. Just say—hook, then—er. You're staring again. Stop it, your eyes are crossing.
WALTER. Excuse me, it's just that it's not every day I sit next to a real live, real live—
LENORE. Hook—then, er.
WALTER. Is it okay if I call you something else?
LENORE. Sweetie, you can call me anything you like. I've been called everything. But I prefer Lenore.
WALTER. Lenore?
LENORE. Yeah, you know, it rhymes with—
WALTER. Don't say it!
LENORE. Will you quit looking at me like that!?
WALTER. Sorry, no offense.
LENORE. You're not offending me, you're making me nervous.
WALTER. The guy who was chasing you then was, was a—
LENORE. A customer.
WALTER. You mean, you and him?
LENORE. You've got it—me and him. Him and me. The two of us! Actually! You just can't be this naive.
WALTER. I'm not, I'm not! I know the score.
LENORE. By the look in your eyes it's nothing to nothing.
WALTER. I know about prostitutes, it's just that I've never ever talked to one before.
LENORE. You want me to say something dirty?

WALTER. Oh no.

LENORE. Don't worry, I won't charge you. I talk dirty for free.

WALTER. I'd rather you didn't, if you don't mind.

LENORE. I know some great words.

WALTER. Please! —Why was that fellow chasing you?

LENORE. Afterwards he wouldn't pay. So, I grabbed his watch and ran out. He chased me into the park. I saw you and you looked like an okay guy, so I made him believe you were my business manager.

WALTER. Business manager?

LENORE. Pimp.

WALTER *reacts, knocks case from bench.*

WALTER. Me!? A pimp? Oh my God!

LENORE. I knew if he thought you were he wouldn't try anything. A lot of the guys carry guns.

WALTER. I knew I shouldn't have bought this jacket. This is awful! A pimp!

LENORE. You're not, so relax.

WALTER. But alluva sudden I feel like one. Seedy, like I've got 8mm films on me. I'll never come to this park again—ever! (*Replaces attache to bench*)

LENORE. Don't take it so hard.

WALTER. It's just the idea, I've never been a pimp before.

LENORE. It's no big deal. You helped me out of a jam, that's all. I appreciate it. In fact, after I fence the watch, I'll split with you. Give me your address.

WALTER. Oh no! Alice would never understand you dropping by the house.

LENORE. Then I'll mail it to you. Cash.

WALTER. I don't want any part of that kind of money!

LENORE. What kind?
WALTER. You know—"that kind."
LENORE. Ohhhhhhh—you mean, "THAT KIND."
WALTER. That's the kind.
LENORE. Look here, baby, money's money. It's all the same, take my word for it. It has no identity, no sex, no conscience, no nationality. It's all green and neuter and beautiful. Now, do you want it or not? Your share will probably be around a hundred. (*She pulls pen, appointment book from her bag*)
WALTER. Don't say MY share! I'm no part of this! I'm clean, an innocent bystander. You keep it all. Spend it on something sensible—like a medical checkup!
LENORE. (*Writing in book*) Fine with me.
WALTER. You're not putting down my name, are you?
LENORE. (*Noting carefully*) Nope, just bookkeeping. "One trick, one watch."
WALTER. It really is a business with you, isn't it?
LENORE. One hundred percent. (*Returns book, pen to bag, withdraws card*) Here. My card, just in case.
WALTER. Just in case of what? I need a hot watch? Forget it! (*Reading card*) Lenore Helms—Interior Decorating.
LENORE. That's my front.
WALTER. Is Lenore Helms your real name?
LENORE. My real name is Martha Snodgrass.
WALTER. Not very exotic, huh?
LENORE. You have to have a star-like name. I've had several. Michelle Landers. Crystal Lee. Stormy Gale.
WALTER. Stormy Gale?
LENORE. That's when I was a nude dancer.
WALTER. In front of people?
LENORE. In front, to the rear, whatever.
WALTER. How could you?

LENORE. For a hundred a night—easy.

WALTER. At the YMCA I couldn't even take showers with the rest of the kids.

LENORE. It's all in how you look at it.

WALTER. Please.

LENORE. A living's a living.

WALTER. You poor thing. I'll feel sorry for you.

LENORE. Do I sense the tone of a missionary? Spare me.

WALTER. Oh no no, it's your life, none of my business. And I can imagine what you've been through. The product of a broken home. An orphan, a waif put out on the streets where you had to fight like an animal to survive. Tragic.

LENORE. For your info, honey, I come from a storybook background in Evansville, Indiana. My mother and father are still happily married, my brothers and sisters look like they've been clipped from Better Homes & Gardens. My dad's an Elk, my mom's in the Eastern Star and my uncle is a big cheese at the V. F. W. post 104. And my childhood was placid and secure and lovely. I never missed a day of school, I was an honor student and I hold the town record of selling more Girl Scout cookies than anyone. And during summer vacations I never ran around with boys—I stayed on my front porch and played Monopoly.

WALTER. Then, tragedy struck. Out of the blue, without warning. Right!?

LENORE. If you can call winning a college scholarship tragedy, yeah.

WALTER. You're college?

LENORE. I have a degree in literature. I was going to be a teacher. But I got bored stiff rotting away in a one horse college town where the hottest spot was the lunch counter at the Trailways bus station. Anyway, the money in teaching is the pits. I got fed up and split for L. A.

WALTER. And that's when tragedy struck.

LENORE. What's it with you and tragedy, anyway?

WALTER. You know—Los Angeles, fast company. Dope.

LENORE. What you been reading? And what's the big deal about L. A.? It's just a spread out Evansville with freeways. And forget dope—I have to keep in top condition.

WALTER. Yeah, I guess you do need endurance. Too bad though, giving up your career.

LENORE. I have a career!

WALTER. I mean, teaching.

LENORE. I am teaching.

WALTER. English!

LENORE. I teach English, too. Two nights a week to a class of slow learners.

WALTER. I thought you said the money was the pits.

LENORE. I don't take money. I do it for fun. And I dig kids. Teaching's a hobby—prostitution's my business.

WALTER. I don't know how you do it.

LENORE. It beats the hell out of pounding an IBM for a hot dog income. And, anyway, I like it. Just think of me as a service organization.

WALTER. Kind of like auto repair.

LENORE. But better. When I give you an overhaul you know you got factory parts.

WALTER. You're actually proud of what you do.

LENORE. Certainly. I'm a reputable business woman.

WALTER. It seems so cold.

LENORE. It is cold. So? When your tailor lengthens your pants you think he falls in love with the cuffs? It's a job.

WALTER. But aren't you ever afraid? Like today?

LENORE. Sure. But that's part of it. Big money, big risks. It goes with the territory.

WALTER. Big money, huh?

LENORE. Yep. And I'm salting away every penny. I'm going to buy an apartment complex. A good return on the dollar and a great tax shelter. I'm retiring in five years. You've got to rake it in while you're looking good. The business is very competitive.

WALTER. Do you ever dicker?

LENORE. I know what I'm worth. No discounts, no specials. Just cash or major credit cards with proper identification.

WALTER. Do you enjoy your work most of the time?

LENORE. Yeah, most.

WALTER. Aren't there some days that you just hate to lie down in the morning?

LENORE. Oh sure . . . I'm human.

WALTER. Then you really like your job.

LENORE. Sure. And I love the money. Do you like your job?

WALTER. I hate it.

LENORE. Whadaya do?

WALTER. I'm in sales. Redwood hot tubs.

LENORE. For some reason it doesn't fit. Like that jacket you're wearing.

WALTER. You don't like it?

LENORE. It's like an ad-on room. Ya know?

WALTER. To be honest I don't feel comfortable in it. I feel big in it, puffy, like one of those Macy's parade characters—obvious. I thought it would be snappy, sharpen up my image. (*Running thumbs under lapels*) Don't you think it says—SALES?

LENORE. You want the truth? It says—yuck!

WALTER. I'm usually basic blue.

LENORE. That fits—that's you.
WALTER. So I've been told.
LENORE. A rule, honey—don't mess with basics.
WALTER. So we're both in sales I guess you might say. Hucksters, peddlers.
LENORE. How's business?
WALTER. Rotten—how's yours?
LENORE. Booming. There's a convention at the Hilton.
WALTER. That's nice.
LENORE. I've only had time for a cup of coffee all day.
WALTER. Really. Gosh. Say, would you be interested in part of a swiss on rye?
LENORE. Sure.
WALTER. (*Snapping open his case*) I hope it's not too dry, I didn't put on a lot of mustard.
LENORE. Don't worry about it. How many tubs have you sold?
WALTER. (*Withdrawing sandwich*) Just one. (*Handing her sandwich*) Here.
LENORE. (*Taking sandwich*) Thanks. Only one?
WALTER. And that was over a month ago.
LENORE. (*Unwrapping sandwich*) How much they pay you?
WALTER. I'm straight commission—six percent. (*Pause, as he watches* LENORE *bite into sandwich*) How's the Swiss?
LENORE. Great!
WALTER. Alice always buys the best cheese.
LENORE. You have any pictures?
WALTER. (*Reaching into inside jacket pocket*) Oh sure. The top of the line is really neat. (*Withdrawing brochure from jacket*)

LENORE. Not tubs—I mean, Alice.

WALTER. Alice? Why you wanna see her?

LENORE. Just curious about the kind of woman who'd let her husband out of the house in a jacket like that. Do you?

WALTER. Yeah—I have a couple on me.

LENORE. Well?

WALTER. I don't know—I feel funny about showing Alice's pictures to a hook and a er—

LENORE. I'll squint—okay?

WALTER. Well—okay. (*Pulling billfold from hip pocket*) These aren't real good, they were taken with a Starflash in a rowboat. (*Pulls photos from billfold, hands them to Lenore gingerly, she notes*)

LENORE. Nice.

WALTER. I'm the one on the right, with the fish.

LENORE. Does Alice still wear bee-hive hair dos?

WALTER. That was taken six months ago.

LENORE. She's a nice looking lady. Kind. Who's the guy in the background in the see-through banlon shirt?

WALTER. Myron—Alice's brother. He still wears those too. He has one in every pastel color.

LENORE. He doesn't look like he feels so good.

WALTER. He'd just sat on a fish hook.

LENORE. (*Handing back photos*) You're a lucky man to have a woman at home like that.

WALTER. (*Taking photos, stuffing them back into billfold*) I wish to hell she was at home, she's out peddling, too.

LENORE. No kidding.

WALTER. (*Replacing billfold to rear pocket*) Real estate. And she just sold her first house. She's doing great.

LENORE. Hey, that's super—that takes the pressure off.

WALTER. Are you kidding!? It puts the pressure on! It makes me feel like a real jerk. She was forced to go to work because I was fired from my regular job.

LENORE. Forced? You twist her arm?

WALTER. No, but if it wasn't for me she wouldn't have to be out—

LENORE. Get off it! I hate guilt.

WALTER. Maybe you have got a good deal. No taxes. Your own boss. No time clocks. No sales meetings. No brochures.

LENORE. (*Finishing off sandwich*) My body's my brochure. (*Balling up sandwich wrapping*)

WALTER. Well, it's about the best sales tool I've ever seen.

LENORE. Why, thank you. (*Tosses paper to ground*)

WALTER. Hey! Stop that! You're littering our *natural environment*. (*He retrieves paper, takes it to trash basket*)

LENORE. Sorry . . . How the hell you expect to sell anything sitting around here? You've got to be out there pitching.

WALTER. I can't take another door in the face. "Hello there, my name is, Walter Price." BANG!!!!! — I'm starting to get oak panel poisoning.

LENORE. You've got to hang in there and pitch.

WALTER. I haven't pitched in over two weeks.

LENORE. You just sit here every day in your horse blanket?

WALTER. Alice and Myron think I'm working.

LENORE. What do you care what they think?

WALTER. It's a matter of dignity.

LENORE. What the hell's dignified about hiding out like a criminal?

WALTER. A guy has to work, or at least act like it.

LENORE. At something he hates?

WALTER. If I did what I wanted — I'd write.
LENORE. So write!
WALTER. There's no future in it.
LENORE. And there's a future in being miserable?
WALTER. And I can't sponge off Alice and take money from Myron.
LENORE. Does he offer?
WALTER. All the time, and I could kill him for it.
LENORE. Did you ever consider he might be sincere?
WALTER. I'm not taking.
LENORE. (*Snatching legal tablet from attache*) Is this your writing?
WALTER. Hey! Put that down!
LENORE. Don't worry, I've washed my hands.
WALTER. Gimme that!!!

LENORE *overcomes his protests, holding tablet close.*

LENORE. C'mon, don't be a knudge! (*Reads*) "On most Saturdays my father took me for a ride in the Dodge. He loved the ocean, so we usually drove slowly along the coast. And, regardless of the weather, he would roll down the car windows in order to commune with the sea. And the great blue-green lady seemed to speak to him in a language that brought him solace, relaxed him, washed away the reality of daily pressures. And thinking back, I can still see him vividly, framed in the open car window against the sea . . . hat back, one foot casually on the dash — smiling." (*Short silence*) Why, Walter, this is real good.
WALTER. Ah.
LENORE. It is! It's warm and real.
WALTER. Just some stuff from when I was a kid. (*Taking back legal pad*)

MAN WITH THE PLASTIC SANDWICH

LENORE. You've got a flair.

WALTER. Ah, c'mon, get off it.

LENORE. You've got a touch. You could develop into one hellava writer.

WALTER. It's just something I've been doing for the fun of it.

LENORE. That's the reason it's got feeling.

WALTER. What the hell you talking about?

LENORE. Because you enjoy it. Can't you see?

WALTER. What I see is that I've got to get a responsible job. I'm not a door to door person, I'm a steady person, a person who shows up and puts in a full day and gets a regular paycheck. I can't sit around scribbling all day while my wife drags clients through houses. God only knows what might happen in some strange bedroom. I've got to get back into the mainstream before it drys up. I need retirement and hospitalization, at my age anything can happen! I've got to get my life together fast, everything's going to hell. Look at me. A year ago a Clinical Engineer, today a pimp! A PIMP! I'm becoming a desperate man. The next time I might keep the watch! My only answer is to get back to work. Then Alice can quit her job and get back to baking sponge cakes. And Myron can take the money he's always trying to lend me and go out and buy the whole rainbow of banlons!

LENORE. Poor little Walter. I'll tellya what, why don't you bring beer here instead of Swiss so you can cry into it.

WALTER. Hey!

LENORE. So you can sit here and feel sorry for yourself.

WALTER. Wait a minute, dammit!

LENORE. (*Overlapping*) So you can sit and blubber.

WALTER. Knock it off! I don't have to—

LENORE. (*Overlapping*) And feel rotten and kick your psyche till it's black and blue!

WALTER. Don't you make fun of me!!! Don't you—

LENORE. (*Overlapping*) The man with the weight of the world in his attache case! With the problems of—

WALTER. (*Overlapping. End of tether.*) World! WORLD! What the, what the hell do you know about the world! The real world of 9 to 5, of people grinding out an honest living and meeting their responsibilities!!!!!

LENORE. You're breaking my heart.

WALTER. People just don't go off doing what the hell they want anytime they feel like it! There are realities, things you just can't turn around like that—(*Snaps fingers*) Some things you just can't change, dammit! I'm sorry my dear Lenore that rhymes with whore, but that's the way it is! Reality, just like I'm a basic blue!

LENORE. It's basic crap! You know who the real whore is here, honey? Not Lenore, no sir, no way. It's good old Walter.

WALTER *begins to gather his materials.*

WALTER. I don't have to take this shit from someone like you! I'm getting out of this crazy place once and for all!

WALTER *slams shut attache.*

LENORE. Go ahead, leave. But if you do you're going to hear me shouting at you all the way across the park.

WALTER *begins to stalk off.*

LENORE. My voice will DEFOLIATE YOUR NATURAL ENVIRONMENT!

This blast stops WALTER *in his tracks. He looks back at* LENORE.

LENORE. Look, I know it's none of my damn business, but certain people have to be told, they cry out to be told. Besides, I'd be shirking my duty as you local hooker if I didn't say something. You, baby, better wake up and shape up and get hold of the beauty in your little blue life. You've got a wife who sounds like a million and a friend who'll gladly give you a million and you, you idiot, are sitting here, hiding out on a park bench. Hell, you've got it made and you're making a mess out of it! Your wife's out working because she wants to help out! You've provided for years so now, when the chips are down, she's out plugging! And you, you won't accept it. Just how the hell you think it makes her feel? Hell man, it's her way of saying I LOVE YOU! And she's probably very happy being a person for a change instead of a sponge cake. And Myron's offering to help you and you won't take because you're too proud. Well, you can take your pride and soak it in your hot tubs — IT STINKS! And you have a flair for writing that's going to waste because of your self inflicted hang-ups. Hell, you've got it all — love, understanding and talent. Man, if I had all the stuff going for me that you do I give up hustling — at least in the afternoons. You've got it made and here you are, sitting around on a park bench, living a lie, dressed up like a carnival barker, blowing it all because of your ego. Well — YOUR EGO'S BULLSHIT!!!!!

Silence. WALTER *stands riveted.*

LENORE. Well, that's it. Now I've got to get back to work. And don't worry, I won't bother you here again. I can't stand the sight of a basic blue blunder. Ciao, honey!

LENORE *exits hastily.* WALTER, *still pondering the impact of* LENORE's *words, stands looking off after her. Slowly he returns to the bench, places attache on its seat, pulls pen and glasses from jacket pocket. He slips on glasses, removes jacket, folds it carefully, places it neatly atop the attache. He takes up legal pad, writes for brief spell. Then suddenly, as if seized by enlightened self committment, he lays pad and pencil aside, stands. He takes up jacket and attache and marches with them to the trash container, slams them into the receptacle with a flamboyant air of defiance. He dusts his hands, returns to the bench, retrieves the legal pad, exits quickly.*

FINAL CURTAIN

PROP LIST

ACT I:

Off Stage:
Walter Price:
>1 black attache case. In case: classified ad section of newspaper, assorted papers, pencils, pens, etc.
>1 brown paper bag containing one plastic cup with coffee, plus lid, and one pastrami sandwich on white wrapped in foil.
>1 pair half-glasses, in jacket.

Ellie:
>1 large canvas tote bag. In tote: 1 carton of yogurt (empty) with plastic spoon attached with rubber band; 1 package of nut-raisin health mix; 1 pair of jogging shoes.

ACT II:

Strike:
>Nuts package, coffee container & lid, paper bag, etc. from trash container.

Preset:
>1 peanut butter and jelly sandwich, partially wrapped in foil. Attache case open on bench, hot tub materials in case and on bench.

Personal Props—Haley:
>Business cards, "Haley Fisk, V.P., G.M., B.R.M. & O."
>Cigar butts. Red bandana, knife, fork, spoon. Salt & pepper shakers. 1 book of matches.

MAN WITH THE PLASTIC SANDWICH

ACT III:

Preset:
    Attache case with want ads, hot tub materials, pens, papers, etc.
    1 yellow legal tablet with story handwritten.
    1 pen.
    ½ Swiss cheese on rye sandwich loosely wrapped in foil.
    Walter's half-glasses.

Off Stage:
Walter:
    1 billfold with family photos for rear trouser pocket.
Lenore:
    1 large shoulder bag containing: address book, pen, compact, business cards reading "Lenore Helms, Interior Decorator."
    1 man's wristwatch.

COSTUMES

ACT I:

Walter Price:
   Dark blue suit, light blue shirt, blue striped necktie, plain black shoes, black hose, black belt, white handkerchief in breast pocket of jacket.

Ellie:
   Bright yellow, youthful dress. Wrist watch.
   Bright yellow tank top and running shorts under dress. High heels.

ACT II:

Walter:
   Same as in Act One except for a bright yellow necktie.

Haley: Old traditional (Brooks Brothers) tweed jacket, pink button-down oxford cloth shirt, tan chino pants, red bandana at neck, work shoes highly polished. Under: faded workshirt, old jeans.

ACT III:

Walter:
   Same as in Act Two except for very bold, mad-plaid jacket.

Lenore:
   Bright, cocktail type dress. Very high heeled shoes. Ornate jewelry.

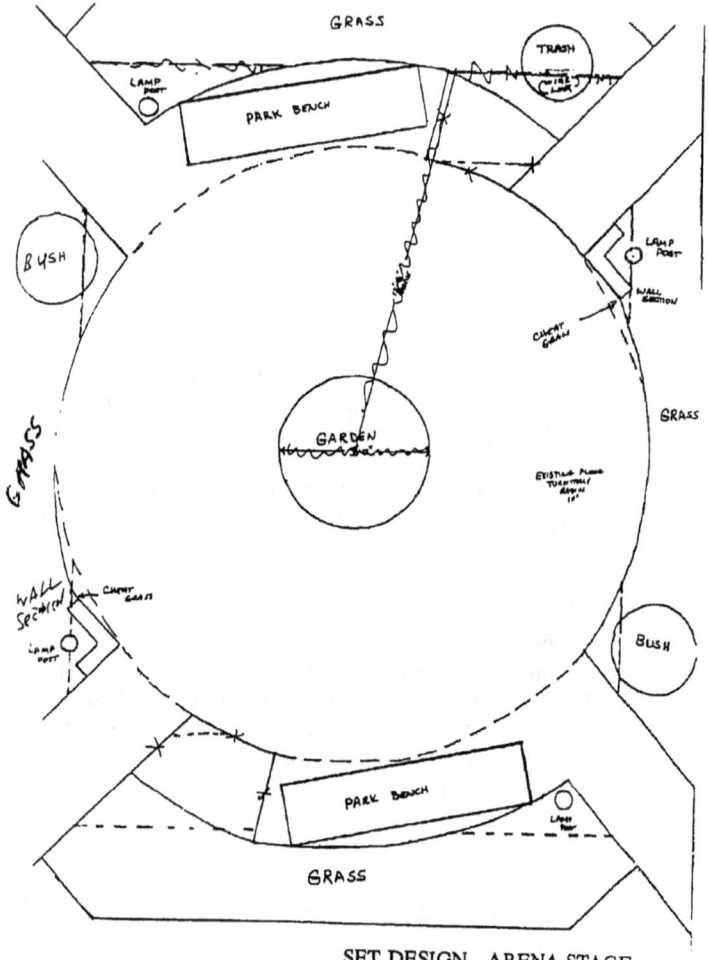

SET DESIGN—ARENA STAGE
"THE MAN WITH THE PLASTIC SANDWICH"

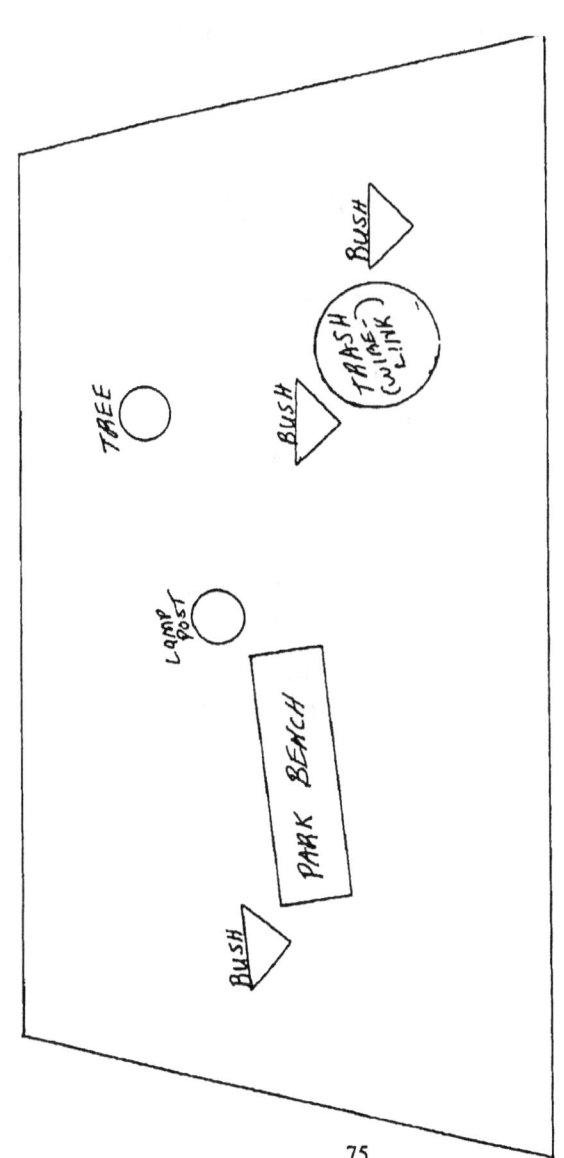

SET DESIGN – PROSCENIUM STAGE
"THE MAN WITH THE PLASTIC SANDWICH"

Also By

Roger Karshner

30 MODERN MONOLOGUES

30 MODERN SCENES

CLOTHES ENCOUNTERS

DON'T SAY GOODBYE, I'M NOT LEAVING

THE DREAM CRUST

HOT TURKEY AT MIDNIGHT

LOVE ON THE CUSP

MONKEY'S UNCLE

TO LIVE AT THE PITCH

WHERE THERE'S A WILL THERE'S A RELATIVE

WHO KILLED THE SAUSAGE KING?

OTHER TITLES AVAILABLE FROM SAMUEL FRENCH

THREE YEARS FROM "THIRTY"
Mike O'Malley

Comic Drama / 4m, 3f / Unit set

This funny, poignant story of a group of 27-year-olds who have known each other since college sold out during its limited run at New York City's Sanford Meisner Theater. Jessica Titus, a frustrated actress living in Boston, has become distraught over local job opportunities and she is feeling trapped in her long standing relationship with her boyfriend Tom. She suddenly decides to pursue her dreams in New York City. Unbeknownst to her, Tom plans to propose on the evening she has chosen to leave him. The ensuing conflict ripples through their lives and the lives of their roommates and friends, leaving all of them to reconsider their careers, the paths of their souls and the questions, demands and definition of commitment.

SAMUELFRENCH.COM

www.ingramcontent.com/pod-product-compliance
Lightning Source LLC
Chambersburg PA
CBHW070648300426
44111CB00013B/2324